MW01710469

HARDPRESS.NET
HOME OF HARD-TO-FIND BOOKS

The Blind Wife, Or, the Student of Bonn

by Thomas Powell

Copyright © 2019 by HardPress

Address:
HardPress
8345 NW 66TH ST #2561
MIAMI FL 33166-2626
USA
Email: info@hardpress.net

WIDENER LIBRARY
HX DNZC 4

DAL 2087.4.75

HARVARD COLLEGE
LIBRARY

BOUGHT FROM
THE FUND BEQUEATHED BY

EVERT JANSEN WENDELL
(CLASS OF 1882)

OF NEW YORK

F. M. Pocock

THE

BLIND WIFE;

OR,

THE STUDENT OF BONN.

To Mrs Brougham
with the Author's regards

THE

BLIND WIFE;

OR,

THE STUDENT OF BONN.

A Tragic Romance.

BY

THOMAS POWELL.

All have—nay, reader, do not start—
A Blue-Beard chamber in the heart.

LONDON:
W. E. PAINTER, 342, STRAND.
MDCCCXLIII.

5

HARVARD COLLEGE LIBRARY
FROM
THE BEQUEST OF
EVERT JANSEN WENDELL
1918

LONDON:
Printed by Maurice and Co., Fenchurch-street.

TO

ROBERT BROWNING,

AUTHOR OF "PARACELSUS,"

This Tragic Romance

IS DEDICATED,

BY

HIS AFFECTIONATE FRIEND,

THE AUTHOR.

THE PERSONS OF THE DRAMA.

The Lady Bertha.
The Lady Julia.
Emmeline, *attendant upon Lady Bertha.*
Wilhelmina, *a Peasant Girl.*
Leonhard, *a Student.*
Fridrich, *his Friend, and cousin to Lady Bertha.*

Wilhelm, Werther, Ernest, Otto,	*Fellow Students.*

Caspar, *Steward to Lady Bertha.*

Conrad, Anselm, Rudolph, Michael,	*Domestics to Lady Bertha.*

Karl, Jarno, Villagers, &c &c.

Scene,—first at Gottingen, afterwards at Bonn.

THE BLIND WIFE.

ACT I.

SCENE I.—*A Club-Room in Göttingen. A number of Students seated,—drinking, singing, &c.*

WILHELM, WERTHER, ERNEST, FRIDRICH, OTTO.

WILHELM.

The great bell is now tolling seven,
And Leonhard is not here. Art sure, good Werther,
He pledged himself to come?

WERTHER.

Sure as I breathe!
Besides he loves so much these merry feasts,
That it could not escape his memory.

ERNEST.

It is his wont
To keep us waiting. There is, methinks, of late
A smack of pride in all he says and does,
As though the applause of those old musty dogs,
The learned Doctors, had destroyed his taste
And relish for the comrades of his youth.

WERTHER.

Nay, he's not proud. 'Tis a mere thoughtless whim,
The love of pondering on stale events
Which concern him not: these make him seem to be
The thing he is not. I have known him long,—
Can well nigh read his thoughts. 'Tis sheer caprice.
No German ever owned a nobler heart,
Nor yet a kinder. All his foible lies
In suffering the excitements of debate
To stir his tongue to speeches, which are his
In words alone.

WILHELM.

He may not come at last;
So let us not delay, but now at once
Proceed to choose another President.
I will propose one. Can we have a better
Than our good comrade Fridrich ?

OMNES.

Agreed ! agreed !

FRIDRICH.

I will not venture to dispute your choice,
Yet merely hold my post till Leonhard come ;
For he may deem me an usurper here,
Having presided at our feasts so long,
And filled the chair with so much wit and worth.

WERTHER.

Not he ! I warrant he'll be glad to scape
The toil of giving out our genial toasts.
Tut ! he is not the jealous pate you deem him.

WILHELM.

I deem him a strange compound, Werther,
A mixture of the lofty and the low;
Full of high soaring fancies, mean delights;
Most inconsistent in his daily life.
I called upon him at his room last week,
And found him plunged in tears! Forsooth the cause,
He had just stumbled on some cruel freak
Played by a tyrant centuries ago.
Then he began forthwith to pour a stream
Of eloquence on man's hard-heartedness,
The daily shower of wrong and cruel deeds
That man deals out to man, and worked his soul
To such a pitch of anger with the world,
I dare be sworn that had he power to do
The workings of his will, he would have sent
The human race, for which he felt so much,
To Hell itself, to learn humanity!
He moralizes if a puppy dies,
And mourns o'er kittens as though he were a cat!
He makes me laugh at all his foolish whims,

And thank the stars I'm no philosopher,
But like the rest of human kind,—a man
Who falls in with the general stream of life,
Nor pours philippics out against the world.

WERTHER.

You fall into our fellow-student's fault,
And rail yourself at him, as he at all
Who bear the shape of Man; which, by the way,
He swears we robbed the injured monkeys of.

FRIDRICH.

Yet has he noble qualities, my friend;
A lofty tongue,—an open generous heart,
Ready to shower his gold on wretchedness!
I know ten thousand generous deeds to speak
Upon his side, and drown your hints of vice.
He is, too, a true German. His eye takes fire
When talking of his Fatherland, and darts
Such glances as would kindle to a blaze
The whole of Germany, had we hearts like his!

And then his passion for the beautiful,—
Who glows like him over our minstrel's song?
You have not walked with him, as I have done,
'Mong silent woods: no idle words are his,
But deep and weighty reasonings on the things
That none, save lofty natures, muse upon:
And in the crowded town his eye is cast
With pondering thoughtfulness on human life,
And all its sad vicissitudes.—But tush!
Let us forego this pro and con, and drink
To Leonhard's health; and would that he were here
To answer for his sins to Wilhelm's face!

[*They fill up, and drink to his health.*

Enter LEONHARD.

LEONHARD.

My loving comrades! I am truly sad
That, by a strange mischance, I missed the hour;
But I am ready to endure your wrath,
And undergo a penance, if it please you.

OTTO.

We will not, Leonhard, lay the blame on you,
But on Dame Fortune, who is blind as Night.
She lost her way,—be all the sin on her.

LEONHARD.

Then Fortune's blindness is her best excuse.
What you call Fortune, some men would call Fate;
And some men call Fate—God! 'Tis well she's blind:
She cannot see the wretchedness we do,
Who have the curse of sight.

OTTO.

Hah! hah! you're in
One of your melancholy moods, forsooth,—
Have seen a charming damsel as you came,
And lost your temper and your way at once,
Because she smiled not on you. Never care
A jot for that: she might be Fortune's self
Whom we have railed at. She is blind, we know,
And could not see your elegance and grace!

FRIDRICH.

Fortune's not only blind, but loves the blind;
For she has showered on a sweet coz of mine,
A gentle girl of scarcely nineteen summers,
So vast a treasury of all that's fair,—
Such virtues, meekness, bland accomplishments,
Joined with such symmetry of form and face,
That Nature must have paused admiringly,
And quite forgot her eyes:—the poor child's *blind!*

OTTO.

Or else in kindness,—lest she should behold
Herself, and pine as young Narcissus did.

WILHELM.

Nay, 'twas in kindness to the general world,
Which had gone mad for such a paragon,
Or brought about another Trojan war.

WERTHER.

'Tis clear she has a Paris in her cousin!
But has she any golden charms as well?

FRIDRICH.

Yes,—that completes the wonder. She is rich
In this world's goods, has large and fair domains,
A goodly castle, too. 'Tis near to Bonn:
The Rhine, our ancient Father, rests his waves
On one side of her lands. But she's the last
Of all her race. Ah! had she but her sight,
She were a wife fit for the Emperor.

[*They all laugh but* Leonhard, *who seems absorbed in thought.*

FRIDRICH.

Nay, you may laugh; but what I've said is true.

LEONHARD.

Enough, good friends. You should not laugh at those
Who suffer from the churlishness of Nature,
Or else for reasons only known to God.
Ere this, the scoffer has been smitten blind,
Or speechless.

OTTO.

Nay, I did not scorn the girl:

'Twas Fridrich's self who moved our laughter thus,
To hear him rant about a sightless child.—
But I must leave you now. I have to meet
Some comrades at a fellow-student's room.
Werther, and Wilhelm too, are bound to go
With me. This meeting has been strangely marred,
Waiting for our wise President, who lost his way!

OMNES.

Then, let us all break up.

[*Omnes exeunt, except* Fridrich *and* Leonhard.

LEONHARD.

There is more sound than sense, my dear friend, Fridrich,
In those good youths: their ears and eyes are made
But for the present and the outer shape.
'Tis strange how differently the same thing strikes
On different men. While they were stirred to mirth
At that young girl's affliction, I could fain
Have given her my own eyes, so deeply went
Your story to my heart. It moved me much.

FRIDRICH.

Ah! and would move you more, could you behold her.
She is the height and paragon of woman!
Her mind excels her outward grace; her heart
Is of God's finest clay, in God's best mould.
I've been her playmate from her infant years,
And all that's good and virtuous in my soul
I've learnt from her,—like to a scentless weed
That, placed against a rose, takes fragrance from
The flower, and has a virtue not its own.
She is a blessing to the neighbourhood,—
A little Providence unto the poor,
Who praise her while the tears stand in their eyes.

LEONHARD.

'Tis strange! You said that she is beautiful.

FRIDRICH.

She has a beauty passing that of woman.
Her form is gently tall, complexion fair
Yet clear as crystal, while the blue veins show

The calmness of the life within ; her lips
Are chiselled by no other hand than God's :
Her light brown hair is braided o'er her ears,
And falls with so much grace, that you would keep
The breeze away lest it should spoil a charm,
Which never could be caught again !

LEONHARD.

You turn
A rhapsodist ; yet I believe each word,
For I have never in my daily life
Heard you o'erstate the simpleness of truth.
But you must love her, by your ardent speech.

FRIDRICH.

I love her as a brother loves a sister,—
Or rather, as a maiden loves a saint ;
But nothing more.

LEONHARD.

My friend, I feel for her

As much as you do, though without knowing her :
For when such gentle creatures visit earth,
They should be treated as we treat a star,—
Looked on with reverence. I shall muse on her,
And make her the companion of my thoughts.

FRIDRICH.

And that will form another bond between us :
Dear Leonhard, I'll out-talk you on that theme,
Nor weary with the toils of victory.
Come let us, ere the sun falls into night,
Take our accustomed stroll, and strive to catch
A glimpse of the great workings of that heart,
Which men do call the [redacted] world.

LEONHARD.

                    The world !
I'm tired of it : it is a nest of sorrow.
To you, dear Fridrich, I unveil myself,
And speak as though I thought aloud. Most men
Have quick, malignant ears to harbour wrong,—

Torturing hypothesis, and making thought
The pandering slave of doubt: that I despise.
But still I venture to impeach the world,
To hold its selfish policy in scorn,
And dare the monster, though I perish for it.

FRIDRICH.

In that you are too rash, and peril more
Than the whole world is worth,—your priceless soul:
For, my dear friend, I have in you observed
A mind that dallies with a mighty fiend.
As yet 'tis unsuspected by yourself:
Be wise, and be less lavish of your doubts
And criminations of the Eternal scheme.

LEONHARD.

You much mistake my meaning; when I gaze
On that drear sea of heaving misery,—
The world in which we live; behold the scorn
Which curls the rich man's lip,—the bitter sneer
Of Mammon, with his heart rooted in gold;

The widow's wrong; the orphan's moan for bread,
With not one raven hovering in the air
To bring the food that once sustained the saint,—
I own my heart grows clamorous with its rage;
And were it not for Jesu's holy faith,
Which holds serene dominion in my breast,
These sights of woe, that from the distant sky
No pitying answer gain,—all these would make
Speech overleap my struggling lips, and shake
The scornful heavens with my discontent.

FRIDRICH.

Nay, be not harsh and violent: all things work
To a good end. We only see the rough
And the wrong side of the world's tapestry.
Be sure of this,—that all is for the best.

LEONHARD.

Dear friend, I hope all is.

[*Exeunt.*

SCENE II.—*Time, Morn.*

An Apartment in the Lady Bertha's Castle. Various Musical Instruments in the Room, Books, &c.

BERTHA *and* EMMELINE.

EMMELINE, *entering.*

Dear lady, here are letters from your cousin.

BERTHA.

They're welcome. Read them, gentle Emmeline:
Thy faithful voice makes kind words doubly sweet,
And I could live on words which breathe of love.

EMMELINE.

And yet you ever smile at love, my lady;
For when I talk of lovers' vows, you shake
Your head, and say, "Though Cupid is a god
Who has no eyes, he does not love the blind."
Ah! I shall live to see you happy yet.

BERTHA.

Happy! My Emmeline, do I seem unhappy?
What do you mean by such a word as that?

EMMELINE.

I mean,—to see you *married.* That's *my* happiness.

BERTHA.

Then go to Bonn, and wed the first you meet.

EMMELINE.

Not without *love.* You spake of love, my lady.

BERTHA.

I see you have mistaken what I said.

EMMELINE.

You said that you could live on words that breathed
Of love:—I think I use your very words.

BERTHA.

They are, but mine is not the *love* you mean.
Not that which makes two selfish bosoms happy;
But that which makes *all* so. The love I had
Within my thought was more akin to his
Who loves all things, though not beloved again;
Who throws from out the fulness of his heart,
And not because he wishes a return;
The love that shines and gives the light, not basks
In others' light. The sun, who floods the world
With such a prodigality of day,
Is happier in dispensing it, than when
He yields the earth to darkness up again;
And I, who never saw his beams, feel this,
And bless him as I feel it.

Do you guess
The love I meant by this rude simile?——
The letter—read the letter: I had quite
Lost that, in setting your stray meaning right.

EMMELINE *reads.*

"Fair cousin, I have written this in haste
To tell you, that a learned friend of mine
(One whom I oft have named to you before,)
Has business that brings him unto Bonn;
Which hearing, I have given him lines to you
Of commendation. He's a noble youth,
And stands the foremost of our College here;
Well bred and gentle, with a depth of thought
Which makes him prized by all. Therefore, sweet coz,
Receive this worthy Leonhard as the friend
Of one who loves you. Farewell: I may send,
Perchance, another letter when he waits
On you at Bonn. Adieu! your cousin, Fridrich."

BERTHA.

There's not a word about himself: of late
His letters have all run upon his friend.
Surely from that he must be truly good,
For Fridrich would not mate unworthily:
He shall indeed be welcome, for his sake.

Before we take our morning walk upon
The terrace looking to the Drachenfells,
Finish the story you read yesternight.

EMMELINE.

Mean you the story of *The Fair Undine?*

BERTHA.

I mean the tale of gentle Juliet.

EMMELINE.

Oh! the play
Written by him whom all the English love?
Lately my lady's heart seems bent to him
Most strangely.

BERTHA.

That Shakspere, Emmeline, is a world to me:
Whate'er is noblest thought is best expressed,
The mind rejoices in his mighty phrase,
Having a robe that's fit to glory in.

The heart gives up its secrets at his touch, —
And at his bidding black Oblivion parts
Her murky waters, yielding up her hoards,—
Letting some captive from the stream emerge,
Like Venus from the waves, as fresh as life.
He, like the fabled king, turns all to gold.
Since I have known him, I have found within
A second being, nobler than the first.
He tops the earth's grand spirits like a god;
And as a mountain rises from the plain,
So he o'er human kind, and soars above
Our common nature.

EMMELINE.

You have a mine of happiness within you,
Filled with rich gems and sparkling rarities,
Which sleep in darkness till some loving chance
Turns up the hidden wonders; then we bless
And prize the earth for such vast treasuries.
I thought, dear lady, music was the world
In which your spirit took its happiest rest?

BERTHA.

Music's one world,—the world of sound; all things
Live in it as an atmosphere: the sea,
E'en in its rudest tempest, has its part
In the eternal pæan, and the wind
Stirs with its mission every leaf,—I know
Even the sounds of silence, far-off heard
In the dim chamber of old memory!

EMMELINE.

The *sound of silence?* Why, that is as strange
As some of Shakspere's phrases. Some would laugh
To hear you say that silence has a sound.

BERTHA.

Well, let them smile: I know full well my thought.
Sometimes I hear, or else perchance I dream,—
(What matter if we hear it when we dream
Or when we wake? the two make up our life,
And one is just as natural as the other,

And both are happy,) sometimes I hear
A song I think my mother often sang.
I turn around; there's no one near,—e'en lose
The sound when listening for it; for it seems
As though it only came when not besought.
Like to a mournful sigh, which from the breast
Steals unawares, so does this music pass
An angel's whisper o'er my tranquil heart.
It is so gentle, that it seems the air:
Earth has no tone betwixt that one and silence.——
I've changed my purpose: fetch the book I named,
And you shall read to me upon the terrace.

[Emmeline *fetches the book. Exeunt.*

SCENE III.—*The Study of Leonhard.*

LEONHARD, *alone.*

So I'm to Bonn by the first light of morn,
With special letters from my trusty friend
To his fair cousin, the blind Lady Bertha;
And he already has despatched due notice
To her of my approach: a rare wild chase.
I know not how it is, but as he speaks
Of this poor girl, I have a thousand feelings
Crowding the portals of my heart: it seems
As though I had an old presentiment,
That she was interwoven with my fate.
Fair, too, and graced with rare accomplishments,
And crowned with large possessions!
Why she's a woman to the very letter;
A contradiction and a paragon.
How is it that I feel this interest
In one I never saw, and never heard of
Till a few days ago? What fantasy

Is playing with the mazes of my will,
And urging me to turn a fool?
Still I must go
To Bonn, and see this marvel of perfection:—
And yet what wild pursuit is this, to run
After a girl that's blind!
What if I marry her?
And Fridrich says she's young and beautiful,
Gentle and good, and blest with wide domains;
Pious, and cheering her benighted state
With all the blandishments that charm in woman.
What if she have no eyes? The more she'll need
The use of mine. How often, as I laid
On sunlit meadows, have I dreamed a life,
And in imagination shaped the world
To my own fancy! Yet, when all flowed on
As I had moulded it, the obstinate doubt
Of something warring with my arrogant will
Made a base discord, and I've sighed to think
How vainly I might try to frame a wife
To be the blessing thought would picture her.

She might, forsooth, have separate joys and tastes,
Loving her independence *like a man,*
Bending her faculties to her own will,
And whistle her obedience to the waves!
But this sweet child must ever lean on me,
And feel I am as needful as the air
Which feeds her life with breath. Nay, I will be
The very breath of her immortal soul!
From me she shall receive the daily stream
Of thought and love, which make up happiness:
Through me she should receive the God of all,
Who died for her! My voice should give her life;
My sight shall pour a landscape of delight.
She shall rejoice that she had never eyes;
She shall be part of all I think and feel.
This would be love indeed, and sweeter far
Than all the common marriages of earth,—
Made up, one half of folly, one of indolence,
Divided selfishness, and egotism,
Each trying to deceive the other; till at last
The lying trick of mutual vanity

Called courtship, is discovered just in time
To know they're wretched, and to feel they hate
Each other, as good politic fools should do.
But this sweet eyeless child of innocence
Shall be a shadow to me. She will grow
Inseparable as thinking to the brain,
And brightness to the sun. Methinks I feel
Her gentle frame resting its blessed weight
On my delighted arm, and with her face
Turned up to feel the rapture of my gaze
Fall on it, as a glory and delight.
How if this be a dream like all the rest
I've laid and dreamed, and woke to find all gone?
Well, let it pass, when I have dreamed it out
Life is a dream of sorrow, joy, and doubt,
And when we wake and find the vision flown,
May we e'en sigh to be in heaven alone!

ACT II.

SCENE I.—*Bonn.—Morning.*

A Room in the Castle.

BERTHA *and* EMMELINE, *seated.*

EMMELINE.

A PERILOUS night we've had. 'Tis many years
Since such a storm has been: the lightning came
In showers of terror, and the thunder broke
Close o'er the castle. 'Twas a selfish deed
To wake you, dearest lady; but that fear
Mastered my reason, and I should have died
If I'd not had your gentle voice to cheer me.
My dearest mistress, do you pardon me?

BERTHA.

I should indeed have deemed you loved me not,
Had you forborne to wake me. I would soothe

Your terror, rather than escape the storm.
The thunder-claps were loud, and I could tell
The flashes were most vivid; for there passed
The dimness of a glory o'er my lids,
Which left a fiery sense. But we must not
Think of ourselves and quite forget the poor:
It must have done some damage to their homes,—
Perchance, which Heaven forbid! have injured some
Of my poor tenants. Send good Caspar forth,
And let him see what aid they may require.
I shall not feel quite happy till I know
I have done all my duty claims of me.

EMMELINE.

Lady, you think so little of yourself!
But God will think the more of you for that.

BERTHA.

Surely the world knows not the crowning joy
Which gentle acts bestow on human hearts,
Or else all would be striving with kind deeds

To put the tyrant Evil down, and raise
A glorious pyramid to their own delight.
Surely no unkind being can be happy,
And kings and conquerors must the madmen be
Who reign by virtue of insanity.
The world knows little of its greatest men.

EMMELINE.

Who are its greatest men?

BERTHA.

The men who walk
In the world's shade, nor court the gaze of man,—
Those who perform their duties gentlest, meekest;
Who, when they're wronged, try not to right themselves,
But leave that unto God, who has declared
"Vengeance is mine,"—yet who, when the proud
And cruel-hearted would oppress the weak,
Stand like a lion in the tyrant's path,
They in themselves bearing and suffering
Till they outwear their persecutor's malice;—

The Saints, who've sown the seeds of Christian faith,
And nourished it with their most righteous blood;—
And next to these the men who stand aloof
From the corruptions of the state, and hand
Their country's freedom down from sire to son:—
Such was our William Tell. To these succeed
The poets, who within their sacred breasts,
Like to the Magians, keep that fire alive,
Which is the beacon to a darkened world.

Enter CASPAR.

CASPAR.

A stranger, bearing letters from your cousin,
Waits in the hall, and now desires to be
Admitted to your presence.

EMMELINE.

Is his name Leonhard?

CASPAR.

I did not ask.

BERTHA.

Inquire his name, good Caspar,
And return. [*Exit* Caspar.
It, doubtless, is my cousin Fridrich's friend.

CASPAR *re-enters.*

CASPAR.

His name is Leonhard, please you, lady.

BERTHA.

Give him admittance ; show him to this room.
Then go without delay to all the villagers,
Inquire what ravages were done last night,
And speedily repair them. Let me know
If the late storm has injured any one.

CASPAR.

I'll lose no time, and will return at noon
To tell your ladyship. [*Exit.*

EMMELINE.

I wonder if this student's a well-favoured man.

Enter Caspar, Leonhard *following, who bows to the* Lady Bertha: *she rises.*

BERTHA.

You're welcome, sir, to Bonn. I have to thank you
For certain letters, which I understand
You have so kindly ta'en the trouble of.

[Leonhard *advancing to* Bertha, *gives* Emmeline *a packet of letters.*

LEONHARD.

I am most proud to be your messenger,
And crave your pardon for this interruption;
But having weighty matters to arrange
In this fair neighbourhood, my bosom friend,
Your cousin Fridrich, honoured me so far
As to make me his poor ambassador,
To tell you, lady, that he talks of you
As of a guardian spirit and a sister.

BERTHA.

Our love is of an ancient date, good sir,
E'en from our cradles.

LEONHARD.

So he's often told me.
You're a theme he never wearies in.

BERTHA.

Sir, he must weary you with such a theme.—
You were not out in last night's storm, I trust?

LEONHARD.

Indeed I was, for I had hoped to reach
Some hostelry before the night set in;
But my poor horse lacked somewhat in his speed,
And ere I reached the inn the storm was done!

BERTHA.

Were you exposed to all its violence?

LEONHARD.

I took some shelter 'neath a forest's edge,
And never felt the regal might of God
So wonderfully grand. The Rhine was lit
With living fire, its waters turned to flame,

And the old castles seemed like blazing ruins.
All was laid bare for miles: darkness and light
Seemed battling for a mastery, and each
Had victory by turns,—now day, now night.
The thunders seemed the angry tread of God
Upon the air, which shrieked with all its might;
While Nature crouched, a living battle-plain,
And shook with dread! My poor steed shivered,
As though it had an ague. 'Twas indeed a storm,
Worthy the very Alps.

BERTHA.

You tell it with a force,
As though you gloried in its perilous grandeur.—
But you require refreshment, and some rest;
I crave your pardon for my want of thought.

LEONHARD.

I pray you will not think of me: I've ta'en
Good care of my poor self. I shall return
To Gottingen within a few short days,

And shall be proud to bear some answer back
To Fridrich, who'll expect it at my hands.

BERTHA.

I trust that while you stay at Bonn, you'll make
This house your resting-place. I shall be glad
To be your hostess.

LEONHARD.

I have not the power
To do such cruel violence to my heart,
As disobey your bidding; though I dread
To trespass on your hospitality.

BERTHA.

I'm happy to bestow this small attention
On my dear cousin's friend.
Good Emmeline,
Bid Caspar show this gentleman a room,
Which he can call his own while he remains
My honoured guest.

EMMELINE.

Sir, will you follow me?

LEONHARD.

Lady, I take my leave, with many thanks.

BERTHA.

I hope to speak with you again to-day.
You can do all that pleases you meanwhile:
Caspar will wait your bidding. So farewell.
[*Exeunt* Leonhard *and* Emmeline.

BERTHA.

That student has a very noble mind.
My ear is quick to catch the soul within
From the tongue's sound, and I have never heard
A voice so full of lofty thought before.
My cousin 's happy to possess a friend,
Who has the noble qualities of Leonhard.

[*Scene closes.*]

SCENE II.—*A Street in Gottingen.*

Enter FRIDRICH *and* WERTHER, *meeting.*

FRIDRICH.

Well met, friend Werther; this is opportune:
I should have else departed from the town
Without one kind adieu.

WERTHER.

Nay, I should then
Have deemed you most forgetful of your friend;
For, to the loving heart, an apprehension
Has all the force of reason, based on none.
What is it that calls you from your studies?

FRIDRICH.

Oh, love! But, thank the stars, my heart is free.
I leave for Bonn to-morrow.

WERTHER.

Our trusty friend,
The moody Leonhard, 's at Bonn.

FRIDRICH.

'Tis his affair
That draws me hence. That studious youth's in love.

WERTHER.

In love? Good Heaven! with whom?

FRIDRICH.

Why I ought scarce
To let the secret out; but in your ear
Once breathed, I dare be sworn 'twere still as death.
Then, you must know, he is in love with one
Whom I have often named to you; a fair
And wealthy girl, a cousin, too, of mine,—
The Lady Bertha: that same sweet blind maiden,
Whose virtues fill the common tongue of Bonn.
I had a moving letter from our friend,

Telling his case, and pressing me with speed
To lose no time, but fly to him at Bonn;
For he was hopelessly in love with her,
And should esteem the minutes long as years
Till he had told her so, and urged his suit.
But this he will not, till he first sees me,
And therefore with the morrow's dawn I start.

WERTHER.

If you're not speedy, he will change his mood;
He ever is in love with some new face,
The last being always fairest, and the best.
I love him much; but were I sire or brother,
He shouldn't wed my sister, or my daughter.
He is too fond of change,—a fickle mind.
Methinks there's madness lurking in his brain:
Be sure you sound him deeply in this fantasy.
Added to this, you ought to bear in mind
The gipsy-girl he took a fancy to,
And purchased of her tribe last year.

FRIDRICH.

Oh, that pretty thing, the melancholy Annette?

WERTHER.

The very same.

FRIDRICH.

But she has long since married.
Surely there's nothing in that idle tale?

WERTHER.

Nothing beyond the rather startling fact
That he became enamoured of her face,
And bought her at a costly price away
From that vile swarthy tribe: then had her taught,
Decked her in finery, made her quite an idol,
And then crowned all this rich absurdity
By marrying her to an honest farmer's son!
Now, I'll be sworn there's something wrong in this.
We do not, in this reasoning world of ours,
Find men so generous, save they have a motive
Which has the serpent—self, coiled in its centre.

FRIDRICH.

You put the worst construction on his deeds,
For, truly, Leonhard loved her as a sister.
Think you, had he a passion for her, he's the man
To let another share the prize he wins?
Nay, 'tis as clear as light to me.

WERTHER.

Well, well! I'll not dispute the point. I own
That I have nothing save a shrewd suspicion,
That will not rest at peace. I wish him well;
But probe his heart most deeply, keenly judge,
And with unsparing tongue strip from his fancy
The gorgeous colours which he weaves around her;
Then if you are convinced he loves your cousin,
I wish them all the joys that wait on love!
Commend me to him. So farewell!

FRIDRICH.

Farewell! You soon shall hear from me again,
If I'm detained at Bonn. Once more, farewell!

[*Exeunt.*

SCENE III.—*A part of Bertha's Domains; Garden, &c.*

Enter BERTHA, *leaning on* LEONHARD'S *arm.*

BERTHA.

I must sure weary you. I can remain,
If you will lead me to a seat, until
You send my faithful Emmeline; who then
Can guide me to the castle back again.

LEONHARD.

Nay, not for all the world. Would that I were
Your Emmeline! to be so needful to you.

BERTHA.

I sometimes fear
Your kindness and forbearance make your lips
Play traitor to your heart. That gentle girl
Has been accustomed for so many years
To be my constant shadow, that I lose
With her the sense of my own helplessness.
Alas! how prone's the human heart to slur

Oppression with the tyranny of custom!
Dear, faithful Emmeline! her love for me
Gives her a strength and patience far beyond
The common energy of life; so pray
Return, and let me ease you of your task.

LEONHARD.

Nay, lady, if that is the only motive,
I pray you let me be your guide for once.
If I have said aught that displeases you,
And for the sin you'd banish me, I crave
Forgiveness.

BERTHA.

I have enjoyed your converse much,
And shall for ever treasure in my heart
This pleasant ramble. Would I had a brother,
Who could, like you, pour floods of light
Upon the darkness of my mind, and make
My happiness twice happier than it is!
We *all* owe God a mighty debt, too great
For words to sum up its amount; but those

Who have the wondrous faculty of sight,
Owe him a greater still. Had I but seen,—
Only for once, the everlasting sky
So full of stars, of which I hear so much,
I could exist upon the memory ;
Or, had I witnessed from the Drachenfells
The silent springing of some golden morn
Which brings the world into the midst of May,—
For well I know that season by the flush
Of odours, which upon my senses steal
Like revelations from an invisible world,
Even as great Columbus felt he drew
To the new world, long ere he saw its groves,
By the land-odours borne upon the wind ;
Or had I gazed upon a human face,
And looked but once on Emmeline's kind eyes,—
I think that would content me : but to be
Shut out from all the glorious works of God,
And at the keenest and the mightiest sense,
Sometimes steals o'er me as a fond regret,
Which leaves a peaceful sadness on my heart.

And yet could I behold the awful book
Of Providence, in which my destiny
Is as a map laid down, I should discern
A special reason for my deprivation,
And have another cause to thank my God!

LEONHARD.

To the contented mind all things *seem* best,
But does not make them so; yet in your case
The sense of sight were a superfluous one:
We can but feel we're happy,—you are so.
The eye is a tormentor when we look
On half the things that strew our daily path.
How else would patient merit know the sneer,
(That loftiest effort of a rich man's mind,
The offspring of his heart,)—or feel the cold
And arrogant smile which strikes into his soul
Like to an icy wind, but for the eye,
That instrument of torture? It had need
Have golden dawns, and night's serene
Magnificence of stars.

BERTHA.

Yet gentle looks
From those we love must be a kind of sky
Which all might *feel*, although they see it not.
I know when others kindly look on me,
And love to keep them near me when I feel it.

LEONHARD.

How could you then, my sweetest lady, wish
To send me from you, if you felt my look ?
For never worshipper gazed on a shrine
With deeper adoration,—purer love,
Than I on you. Pardon me for this speech :
It is too bold, but ere I knew the sound
And meaning of my words, they had escaped.
Your pardon, gentle lady.

BERTHA.

Pardon, my kind friend?
Pardon for what ? That you are good to me,
Feel pity for me, and express it kindly ?

LEONHARD.

Oh, Lady Bertha, gently bear with me!
And if my words offend your saintly ears,
And seem less reverent than a worshipper,
Say so, and I am dumb for ever. But my heart
Holds a great secret, which I must impart.
Will you please sit upon this grassy bank;
The trees have kept it dry: and then—

Enter EMMELINE.

Oh, fatal interruption!— [*Aside.*

EMMELINE.

Dear lady, I have come to tell you news.
A messenger has arrived to say your cousin
Will speedily be here, to rest awhile
From academic labours. I am out
Of breath; for I have run to tell you this,
Knowing the joy it would occasion you.

BERTHA.

That is joy indeed. I will return

Straight to the castle. Gentle sir, I now
Release you from your task, and thank you much
For your most careful guidance: till evening comes,
Farewell! I shall expect you in the room
Where are my books and music. So farewell!

[*Exeunt* Bertha *and* Emmeline.

LEONHARD, *alone*.

Another instant, and the secret had
Escaped me, and for ever. On a word
I should have perilled my life's happiness!
Mad gambler that I am, to risk at once,
And on a sudden impulse, all my hopes,—
That impulse, too, founded perchance upon
A misconception! Only three days here,
And hazard all so rashly: mad, fond fool!
Had I avowed my love, moved her displeasure
At my presumption, all had then been lost!
That lucky—that felicitous intrusion
Of her attendant, has most likely saved me.
I think, if I can read the heart aright,

And catch a meaning from the human voice,
She loves me: yet that may be a mere fancy.
I'm glad the secret's safe till Fridrich comes:
Surely he'll not oppose—nay, he'll aid me;
Will urge my suit, perchance, with his fair cousin.
He can say more for me than I should like
To plead upon my own behalf; and he is true.
Yes, I can trust him!

But he tarries long.

How slowly time and friends lag on our biddings!
When we are sailing on the sea of love,
And driven onward by our full-sailed hopes,
Time's measured more by thought than by dull sand,
Which takes no quickening pulse from bounding hearts.
Should he delay his coming till to-morrow,
Can I keep down the impatience of my soul?
No! I must know my fate.

Enter FRIDRICH.

Fridrich, the words are warm upon my lips,
Which blamed you for your tardiness; yet now
I feel reproach for my unthankfulness.

Ten thousand thanks for your most welcome presence !
Have you but just arrived ? or have you seen
Your gentle cousin, the sweet Lady Bertha ?

FRIDRICH.

I have not seen her yet ; and ere I do,
I must confer with you upon the matter
Which brought me hither. You're in love with her,
For you could never write me so in jest.

LEONHARD.

Fridrich, I never, till I saw her, knew
What true love was. If other forms remained
Lingering upon my memory, they have gone,
Like a pale star before the sun's great birth.

FRIDRICH.

How often, Leonhard, have you said the same ?
Those similes roll right smoothly from your tongue,
Which seems well tutored, and the emphasis
Is laid upon the most appropriate word ;

While your looks match it with that wondrous grace,
Which practice only can acquire, and skill
May challenge as the triumph of its art.

LEONHARD.

Oh, Fridrich ! will you urge a querulous quirk
Against the deep-toned passion of a soul,
Which never felt its craving amplitude
Filled up till now ? The smiles of other eyes
Were but the dawning of that day of love,
Of which she is the sun : and shall a cold
And heartless logic rob me of the light
Which I must have, or perish ?

FRIDRICH.

My dear friend,
Those hymns have oft been sung to other ears ;
Yet they have passed away, and you have lived.
Methinks you are immortal in your love,
And feel no sorrow when a woman dies ; —
But place, forthwith, another on her throne,
The heiress and successor to your heart.

LEONHARD.

Why do you try me thus? If but in jest,
You trifle with a heart which never yet
Has trifled with another's,—one that has felt
More for the meanest beggar than itself.
I think that I may say you trifle with
Two hearts, for I believe your cousin loves me.

FRIDRICH.

Mistake me not, good Leonhard: you must feel
I have a sacred duty to perform. Think not
That I have laid so near your heart to wring
Its closest secrets out, and then betray you.
But you've confest to me you oft have loved
Before you came to Göttingen, and that
In Rome you whiled the sunny hours away
With a fair damsel, one Florentia;
And that you left the eternal city's gloom
Stricken in spirit, broken down in heart,
Shattered in frame, when the sweet jade left you
To run away with some rich English lord!

You came to Gottingen: while there you've passed
Some pleasant hours, forsooth, with other dames,
And been a general lover. Werther says
You are as fickle as an April day,
And change more quickly than the summer's wind,—
Ever in love, and ever out of it.

LEONHARD, *after a pause.*

'Tis true,—I own it all: for I have been
In quest of my life's hope; which to attain,
Would in that moment all past time redeem,
And bring the heaven I dream of to my grasp.
Fridrich, I've ever been in search of that
Which I have found in this all-matchless creature,
Your gentle cousin Bertha,—the other half
Of my immortal spirit; for I hold
That every human spirit is twin-born,
Formed in a vast and pre-existent state,
But separated ere they reach this world:
And some are doomed to meet again on earth,
Where they incorporate, and thence become

Indissoluble in eternal bliss.
This is a truth I firmly hold, and she
Is that one spirit sought. Her voice will fill
My heart with music, and my soul with joy;
Her love sustain me; while the sense of sight,
Which Nature (else too prodigal to one
So framed and steeped in beauty) has denied,
Gives her a claim resistless on my heart.
I need not paint her beauty unto you,
But ah! she seems to me divine; and when
She speaks, I deem some radiant angel opes
Ambrosial lips, and fills the panting air
With all the precious harmonies of thought.

FRIDRICH.

Nay, that is frenzy.

LEONHARD.

Then if love be frenzy,
I have been mad from birth; for from the first
I had a craving for a kindred heart,

And my soul panted with unearthly thirst
For that deep draught of love, which never yet
Has met this lip till I beheld your cousin!
When I was quite a child, my heart was given
To one as young,—a fair-haired girl, whose years
Had not told seven; and we passed each day
As though we were alone in paradise;
Hand locked in hand, and eyes deep fixed on eyes,
And breast to breast, feeling each other's heart
Pulse against mutual bosoms full of peace.
We told each other every thought we had,
Fresh as it sprang; and if one ceased
To look upon the other, we have wooed
The vagrant eyes until they met again.
And if one smiled, the other also smiled:
One feeling flowed through both our youthful breasts.
We roved the fields together, and the birds
Sounded to both alike. Her name e'en now
Revives within me every bygone scene,
With all its music crowding on my heart.
I see them all, like to a flash of thought

Which in an old man's memory lights up
The scenes of early youth: now all are gone.
Or as I once remember, in a storm,
When the dark clouds dashed fiercely at the earth,
A flash of lightning laid the whole plain bare;
Tower, hill, and village spire stood out in light,
But in an instant all was dark again.
Well, we were torn apart by daily life,
And parted ne'er to see each other more!
But she was ever music to my thought,
And I have often moved myself to tears
By musing on her form, which grew divine
Beneath the sanctifying power of love.
Full twelve years afterward I chanced to stray
With a young fellow-student, till we found
Ourselves within a churchyard. "Ah!" said he,
"In this secluded spot a gentle form
Is slowly mingling with the common dust:
She was the bosom friend of a dear sister,
Herself now gone to rest. This gentle girl
Was full to bursting of all beauteous thoughts,

And fair as she was gentle." I was moved
By the deep pathos of his mournful voice,
And asked that he would show me where she slept.
He led the way. I, in prophetic grief,
In silence followed. "Here," said he, "she rests."
I looked, and darkness came— [*after a pause*]
for 'twas *her* grave.

FRIDRICH.

I've heard you tell that moving tale before,
And wept when it was told. I do not hold
Your love the lighter in my mind's esteem,
Because your heart loved from its dawn of feeling;
But rather deem it a sure pledge that you
Will love unto the end. Dear Leonhard,
Within the faithful circle of my soul
No comrade holds so high a place as you;
And we have singled from the crowd apart
Each other as companions, and true friends.
I know your noble nature well, and feel
A brother's love for you, as well as Bertha.

But can you wed a helpless thing like her,—
A constant drain upon your daily thoughts?
Pause, ere you tear her from a virgin state,
Full of the sweetest sanctities of peace,
And tempt her to a life more full of care
And peril than the present. Oh, beware
How you take on yourself a perilous weight,
Which only love can bear. Think of her then,
Lonely beyond the desolate Carthage shore,
Whose former glory made the ruin deeper,
Should you erect upon her vestal heart
A glorious temple, there enthrone a god,
And when her trusting heart had learned to worship,
Despoil it of its deity, leave it bare,
Dismantling it of glory, like a shrine
Mournful in ruin, silent—dark as night.

LEONHARD.

Do you look on me as a man or fiend?
None, save a fiend, could hurt that gentle girl,
And I would wear my life out to avenge

The slightest wrong that aught would offer to her.
If you do love me, you will trust me now:
I pledge myself to watch her night and day,
And she shall be the world in which I live.
Oh, what a joy to guide her gentle steps
To some fair mountain's height! and while we sat
Together in its quiet, I would pour
The glory which slept round us in her ear,
And paint the castled Rhine, and make its halls
Festive with mirth again!
Tell how the maiden loved, and warrior died
Triumphant in his pangs, and awing Death,
Which bowed beneath its victory!
And when the Spring,
With all her fragrant odours on the wind,
Came like a breath of life, oh, what delight
To lead her where those gentle breezes stir,
And let her cheek receive them! When away,
My soul should to its deepest haunt retire,
And there relapse into a trance of prayer,
Kneeling before her form as to a shrine,

While it, a fond idolater, bowed down
And worshipped in the silentness of joy!

FRIDRICH.

I have performed my duty, have warned you
Of all a jealous fancy could devise,
And will not stand between your happiness.
Only on one condition will I ask
The lady Bertha,—to which pledge yourself:
That if she should decline your suit, you straight
Leave Bonn, and never urge your love again.

LEONHARD.

Most cheerfully: my pride would scorn to sue
Twice to one lady.

FRIDRICH.

Then, my friend, adieu!
I'll seek my cousin, and will urge your suit.

LEONHARD.

Oh, may thy voice be soft as Orpheus' lute! [*Exeunt.*

ACT III.

SCENE I.—*An Apartment in the Castle.*

EMMELINE *alone, arranging some books.*

'Tis very clear my lady loves this student;
But her dear innocent heart yet scarcely knows
That which I'm sure of. As he touched her hand
Last night, her frame shook with her beating heart:
That's a sure sign of love; and when she speaks
To Leonhard, her tone is altered quite,
And has a trembling music like a song
That's broken with the passion of the singer.
Surely, she ne'er could meet with one more worthy.
He has a kind, a noble generous look,
While she is beautiful beyond all girls
That I have ever seen: her want of sight
Will give her a fresh claim upon his heart,
And make her love him more for that attention
Which he will pay to her.

Enter CASPAR.

CASPAR.

I thought the Lady Bertha had been here.

EMMELINE.

Your lady's with her cousin on the terrace.
What is it that you want?

CASPAR.

Oh! Wilhelm's son
Has brought a nosegay for her, and has asked
For leave to give it to her hand himself.

EMMELINE.

Then let him wait till I have told her so.

CASPAR.

He'd better come some other time; and yet
It will displease her gracious heart to send
Even a beggar away. He'd better wait.

[*Exit* Caspar.

Enter LEONHARD *and* FRIDRICH.

FRIDRICH.

Your mistress wishes you to go to her.
You'll find her in the music room.

[*Exit* Emmeline.

LEONHARD.

Fridrich, I feel too happy. Dearest brother,
You are my benefactor, more than friend;
That sounds not deep enough. How can I pay
Even a tithe of the vast debt I owe you!

FRIDRICH.

One way alone can pay me,—more than pay me,
And make me turn the debtor. I have given
A pearl to you beyond all human price—
Almost have been the surety for your love;
And though she owned she loved you as a friend,
Yet frankly she confessed her doubts if you,
So full of active faculties, could tie
Yourself to one so helpless as herself.

Therefore I am your bondsman, noble Leonhard.
Love her, and be all you have said you will,
And Páradise owned not a happier pair.

LEONHARD.

My life will show this;—and in after times,
When you are here, I'll tell the pleasant tale
That you mistrusted me;—'twill make her smile.
My fault will be upon the other side:
I rather fear that my assiduous care
Will weary her of me.

FRIDRICH.

I shall be well content to blame her then.

LEONHARD.

Come with me, dearest Fridrich, to your cousin,
That I may pour out my full heart before you,
And swear allegiance to its sacred queen.
Farewell the troubled life! henceforth the pure, serene!

[*Exeunt.*

SCENE II.—*The Terrace.*

Enter BERTHA *and* EMMELINE.

EMMELINE.

The joy of those we love is sweeter far
Than our own selfish pleasures, dearest lady;
And yet I feel half sorrowful with hope,
Like flowers that, overladen with the dew,
Droop 'neath their sparkling burden.
I am glad your wedding is to be so soon.
Love at first sight, and marriage the next day, —
This is the true philosophy of love!
I hate long courtships, for affection cools
In that probation: there is just enough
Of time to find the smallest foibles out,
And not endear the woman.

BERTHA.

You are sure
To say that I am right in all I do:

'Tis well to have such gentle monitors.
But, Emmeline, in this step I have been
Guided, as usual, by my cousin's counsel:
He has confirmed my heart in this fond choice.
When first he spoke of Leonhard, I felt
A strange and growing interest in his fame;
But when I heard his voice, it seemed to fill
The yearning cavern of my heart, and make
My soul alive with music. I am blest
In one so learned, noble, and devout.
You, also, will be happier for our marriage.

EMMELINE.

I shall be happier, if you are so.

BERTHA.

I hear a gentle footstep drawing near,
And by the music of the pace I know
It is my own kind Leonhard. As the air
Feels by its radiant flutter that a star
Is journeying in its space, e'en so do I

Know by the rapture stealing o'er my soul
That his glad presence, like a brightening dawn,
Fills all with joy and light!

Enter Leonhard *and* Fridrich.

LEONHARD.

My sweetest Bertha!—
Nay, Emmeline, that charge is mine: her arm
Goes with her heart.

[Bertha *takes the arm of* Leonhard.

You lean too lightly on my arm, dear Bertha;
I scarcely feel the pressure.

BERTHA.

The lightest yoke is always longest borne.
That is a maxim with your politicians.

LEONHARD.

Our rulers seldom act upon their maxims.
They seem to think the heavier they load
The German heart, 'twill bear oppression longer.

FRIDRICH.

Dear Bertha, let not Leonhard's fiery faith
In the *impossible*, convert your heart
Into a nest of stinging discontents.
Our rulers are but men; doubtless they err,
But we should stray as widely from the path
Of wisdom, were we steering in their place.
The world's a waste of waters, full of rocks,
With smiling visions of delightful isles,
Where plenty ever reigns and music plays,
Where fond ideal lovers live on sighs,
And wed on unsubstantial happiness!

LEONHARD.

Truce to your banter, Fridrich! Future Time,
Which e'en now raises its immortal wing
As though about to soar, will bear us on
To a far better state; where *Hope* shall stir
The wishes of a poor man's heart, and give
To him a vigour worthy of the age
When conquerors were taken from the plough.
And yet I should be loath to drag our ploughmen

To such a degradation! Swords become
Mere butchering knives, when with the plough compared.
No: Cincinnatus was a man indeed,
When he threw off the long and sable locks
From brows thick sweated with his daily toil;
But dwindled to a conqueror, when he came
Back from his victory.

Enter CASPAR.

CASPAR.

Here's Karl, my lady: he has brought a nosegay,
Which he requests to give to you himself.

BERTHA.

I will receive him now.

[*Exit* Caspar.

LEONHARD.

To bring some flowers
Ah! ah! there's something hidden in those flowers;
No serpent, Bertha, but a sly petition.
Well, that's a flowery way of asking favours,
And like a rose which has the thorn concealed.

BERTHA.

Wait till he come. I often have these presents.

Re-enter CASPAR *with* KARL. Karl *bows, and going up to* Bertha, *kneels, and presents the flowers.*

BERTHA.

Thanks, my good Karl;—but, surely, you have taken
More trouble for me than you need have done.
I hope your aged father's well, and that
You all are happy.

KARL.

Please you, my father's well
So are we all,—but I 'm not very happy.

BERTHA.

Not happy! What is the cause of that?

KARL.

I came to tell you, lady,—for I know
That you do all you can to make us happy,—
Jarno is going to marry Wilhelmine;
Yet she loves me, and I also love her

BERTHA.

Why then, good peasant, does she wed with Jarno?

KARL.

Her father makes her marry him, because
Jarno has got a farm, and I have not.
I know 'twill break my heart, and Wilhelmine's;
But neither Jarno nor her father care for that.

BERTHA.

Nay, never would a parent do so harsh
A deed, as make a daughter miserable!
I will send Caspar to him, and desire
That he will come to me; then if I find
That Wilhelmine loves you, and that the case
Is as you state, I'll grant to you a farm,
And surely then her father will consent.

KARL.

God bless you, lady! I will pray for you,
To my last day on earth!

BERTHA.

Good Caspar, go
And bid the young girl's father wait upon me
This evening at the castle, with his daughter.

[*Exit* Caspar *and* Karl.

LEONHARD.

Dear Bertha, I must share these duties with you,
And be the instrument of your bounteous nature.
Your life is a sweet round of charities,
Which makes me think you are a blessèd Spirit,
Sent here to minister to wretchedness.
I shall forget you are a gentle maiden,
And look on you as a divinity!

FRIDRICH.

The air is growing somewhat damp and chill;
So let us to the castle.

[*Exeunt.*

SCENE III.—*A Cottage.*

Enter from it WILHELMINE.

WILHELMINE.

I hope Karl will carry the nosegay carefully to our lady. I hope he will, for I never took more pains to place my curls right when Karl first came to make love to me, than I did in putting those beautiful flowers into their prettiest shape. Oh, the pains I took!—first a rose, then a geranium, next a laburnum falling over it like a shower of gold; now a piece of sweet-briar, beside that some carnations, violets, heliotrope, myrtle, and hyacinth; then the pet of my garden, a passion-flower. I cried when I gathered that, for my sweet little Claudine gave it me just before she died; but I would give my heart to our lady;—nay more, I think I would give my eyes to her! Alas! she will not be able to *see* the care I have bestowed on that nosegay; but she can smell the *fresh flowers*. I am so glad she likes the smell of flowers: oh, it is better than *looking* at them. I should like to see the student she is going to marry; it is so like an angel, as our lady is, to marry a poor man, if he be only a good and kind one! If I were a lady and had a castle, I would marry Karl to-morrow; and I would scold my father,—and I'd have Jarno tossed in a blanket, too. I'd make him marry old Bridget, that I would, and she would lead him a nice life. He'd repent as long as he lived having teased me, and telling tales to my father against Karl. Oh, he's a wretch to think, because he has a farm and Karl has none, that he will terrify me into marrying him. I won't, that I won't! I'd sooner die an old maid!

Enter JARNO.

Here he is. Well, I must not be rude to him; but I will not be very civil.

JARNO.

Dear Wilhelmine, I am so glad I have found you alone

WILHELMINE.

I am not *alone*, as it happens.

JARNO.

Not *alone!* Why, is Karl here? or your father?

WILHELMINE.

Neither.

JARNO.

Then you must be alone.

WILHELMINE.

No, I am not. You are here,—so I'm not alone.

JARNO.

Ah! ah! ah! But I did not *find myself* with you. I came to you; so I have you there. Ha! ha!

WILHELMINE.

If you came to laugh at me, it is very rude; and I will tell my father, as well as Karl.

JARNO.

I hope I have not made you angry?

WILHELMINE.

Why are you glad I am alone? You are not going to kill me, I hope; for you look so wildly at me.

JARNO.

I want to tell you something.

WILHELMINE.

Cannot you tell my father? for I don't wish to hear any thing you have to say.

JARNO.

I am sure it will please you.

WILHELMINE.

I am sure it won't.

JARNO.

Yes it will. Dear Wilhelmine, I love you

WILHELMINE.

Well! what of that? You don't say that half so *well* as Karl.

JARNO.

I don't like him.

WILHELMINE.

I *do*.

JARNO.

I am sure you would like *me* better, if you would only try.

WILHELMINE.

But I won't *try*.

JARNO.

Your father, who is much wiser than we are, says you *ought*, and that he will make you.

WILHELMINE.

Then you had better make love to a *wise* woman, and not a young one, since you talk of wisdom. So you can make love to *my* old aunt Bridget: she is a treasure of wisdom.

Enter KARL; *not seeing* Jarno, *he runs up to* Wilhelmine, *and kisses her*.

WILHELMINE.

Oh, fie! Karl; I am so angry with you.

KARL, *seeing* Jarno, *looks abashed.*

Why, Jarno, what brings you here?

JARNO.

I came to see Wilhelmine's father.

WILHELMINE.

Have I not told you my father is not here? so you had better go.

JARNO.

I will go, certainly; but I shall tell your father of what Karl did. I am shocked that any young woman should let a man kiss her. Indeed I am shocked!

[*Exit* Jarno.

WILHELMINE.

Now, Karl, what does our lady say?

KARL.

Oh, she is going to give me a farm.

WILHELMINE.

You must come into the cottage, dear Karl, and tell me all our lady said to you

KARL.

Oh, we shall be so happy!

[*Exeunt.*

SCENE IV.—*Villagers, with Garlands of Flowers, the Peasants in their holiday Clothes. A triumphal Arch of Flowers. A Band of Musicians.*

Enter CASPAR, *and the Domestics of the Castle. Villagers go up and congratulate* Caspar, *and shake his hand.*

CASPAR.

Thanks, my good friends—but don't stand in the way. Your lady and Count Leonhard will be here

Almost upon the instant. Group yourselves,
And make a line for them to pass.

FIRST VILLAGER.

Ah, that Leonhard is a goodly looking man!

CASPAR.

Count Leonhard, you should say; for as he marries
My lady, he will be a Count. Now don't forget
To call him so. Stand back: our lady comes.

Enter Bertha, Count Leonhard, Fridrich, *and* Emmeline; *they pass into the church. Villagers group. Scene closes.*

NOTE.

year is supposed to have elapsed between the third and fourth Acts.

ACT IV.

SCENE I.—*Count Leonhard's Study.*

LEONHARD, *alone.*

WE are the slaves of circumstance, and bend
Beneath the constant pressure of its weight;
Thus we become, and imperceptibly,
The contraries to ourselves. Who would have dared
To tell me, when I married Lady Bertha,
That in a little year I should retort
Upon my heart the folly of that choice!
Yet she is still the same: 'tis I alone
Am altered. She is far too pure to change!
All natures that are mixed must needs become
Better or worse. There is no pause in life,
Either in form or heart: downward we tend,
Or else aspire. Man has no resting-place,

Till he has reached the first stage in his being,—
The silent and mysterious grave. The Spring
Is here again: the leaves throng on the trees
As to a festival; the flowers have heard
A voice call to them from the breezy air:
But I have somewhat dulled the sense of joy
In changing seasons, since this ill-starred marriage!
All seasons are the same to me. How soon
I felt that helpless creature was a task!
Now Julia is indeed a noble prize;
She's worth the winning, and the wearing too.
Her form is not perhaps so faultless as
The shape of Bertha, and her voice may want
The silver tones of that meek paragon;
Yet she's a woman that a king might love,
And glory in his conquest. Her sweet breast
Rises and falls like to a heaving wave,
When mirth or music stirs her passionate soul!
And then her eyes—great God! they make me feel
Faint with love languishments. I'll con no more
Her beauties over, lest I should grow mad

With my desire, and lose the guide of reason.
Oh, that she were my wife instead of Bertha!
Or, that she had been staying with her friend,
When my unlucky footsteps roved to Bonn!
What a sweet dream was that of yesternight!
Methought that I was wedded to this Julia,
And when I asked where Lady Bertha was,
They told me she was dead; and I felt happy,
As though a weight had fallen from my heart.
That dream may be prophetic. I have known
Such dreaming fancies of the brain result
In marvellous fulfilment. One at Rome,
The night before I was to meet Bianca,
Preserved me from the bravo's searching steel.
And then my vision in the Coliseum!
Tired with the sultriness of day, I sat
Upon a fragment of that mighty ruin,
A landmark in oblivion's shoreless sea,
When sleep fell o'er me. Sudden as a thought
Before me stood, in their half-demon robes,
The Grand Inquisitor and all the fiends

That follow at the Roman priesthood's heels.
I felt as on a rack, limb wrenched from limb;
Stretched to that point when life just lingers on
Only to feel its agony, and too faint
To bear the torture like a man. I thought
They put a monstrous engine on my head,
Which slowly crushed the bone into my brain,—
Then all was over: I was dead—was free!
The torture woke me, but the fear remained;
And ere the day had pass'd into the night,
I was upon the road to Germany,
And learnt, by letters from Italian friends,
That very night Rome's hell-hounds in full cry
Were after me, as a foul heretic!
And other dreams of mine have often been
The heralds of events. So this may prove,
And Julia with her world of living charms
May yet one day be mine. Delicious thought
I feel her melting in my amorous arms,
And kissing me away into a trance!

Enter JULIA.

LEONHARD.

Are you fair Julia? or a pictured thought
Of the sick brain, which makes a vision stand
Before it, painted in the crystal air?

JULIA.

What fond conceit is that, Count Leonhard?
I came to you as an ambassador
From your fond wife.

LEONHARD.

What is it she wants with me?
Must I for ever follow at her heels?

JULIA.

Nay, be not so displeased; I came from her
With a love message.

LEONHARD.

Then, for the music of your own sweet lips,

Tell me the message; and for your sweet sake
I will be patient, though it last a year.

JULIA.

It will not last a minute; she requests
That you will join her in the music-room.
She is not well to-night.

LEONHARD.

She's never well.
It is a mere pretence! But I will go
At my first leisure. [Julia *going*
Nay, leave me not, sweet Julia;
I have a message for you. I received
Yours patiently; so listen now to mine.

JULIA.

I cannot listen now.

LEONHARD, *detaining her by the hand.*

Nay, for an instant.

JULIA.

I will return: but first I must despatch
Some letters to my friends at Heidelberg.
My visit here is now so near its close,
I dare not lose a day,—nay, not an hour,
Or else at home they will be unprepared
For my reception.

LEONHARD.

Wherefore leave the castle?
Let me entreat you to prolong your stay.

JULIA.

I may revisit you next Spring; my brother
Has just arrived from Spain, and writes to me
In such a moving fashion, I can find
No motive for denial.

LEONHARD.

May I see
This urgent letter?—that is, if it bear
No secrets, fairest Julia.

JULIA, *giving the letter.*

Here it is.
Restore it to me when we meet at supper;
Till then, I say adieu! [*Exit.*

LEONHARD, *with the letter in his hand.*

She says 'tis from her brother.
When did a sister ever show such haste
To obey a brother's whim. [*reads.*
"Dear Julia,
My kind and gentle sister,"—(ah! forsooth,
He calls her sister,)—"I have just returned
From Barcelona, and I long to see
Your merry face again; so prithee lose
No time, but haste to Heidelberg. I bring
A prize with me, worthy a German girl,—
A rich young nobleman of Arragon.
So haste to meet your brother, and if that
Be not enough to stir a sister's heart,—
A handsome lover! Your fond brother, FRANZ."
This blows my scheme to air! What scheme had I?

None: I should say, my dream. Then all is lost:
I will at once search Julia out, and own
My love. Perhaps this is a plot of hers,
To quicken me to action. She may think
I love her; and who knows a woman's heart
So well, he may not be for once deceived?
Julia may not be quite invincible.
But I must first to this meek wife of mine.
Oh, that she were an angel—not a woman!

[*Exit.*

SCENE II.—*An Apartment in the Castle.*

BERTHA, *seated.*

I never felt so sad as now: 'tis sure
The lingering memory of last night's music.
There was too much of melancholy in it:
That ballad of the girl who died for love,
Slain by a cruel lover, haunts me still.
We scarcely know the gifts that bless us most.

When first I thought my Leonhard's voice betrayed
His love for me, I blessed that fine keen sense
By which I caught the assurance; but, alas!
'Tis now as quick and sensitive to detect
His altered manner. All his words are still
The very same, but they have lost the tone
Of tenderness which made them precious to me.
How soon he felt I was a toil to him!
Scarcely four months had passed, and he gave o'er
Those readings which were life to me; our walks
Became less frequent; then came Julia,
My dear, kind kinswoman,—that seemed to spur
My Leonhard's apathy. Our pleasant walks
Were quick resumed; again he read to me,—
I should say read to *us*, for Julia's wit
And happy manners pleased dear Leonhard much,
So that fresh joy was mine when first she came.
But now she hastens back to Heidelberg,
Though I have urged her all I can to stay;
Yet, as her brother has returned from Spain,
'Twere selfish to importune her so far.

Oh, I must be a weary task to Leonhard,—
Indeed to all. It was so like a child's—
The thought he would devote his active mind
To watching o'er a helpless thing like me.
Ah! should this weariness increase upon him,
I have lived too long. O dreary days to come!
And drearier years! [*She bursts into tears.*

Enter LEONHARD; *he stands looking on her for a time.*

LEONHARD.

In tears again, my Bertha! Seldom now
Smiles beam on me. What idle whim is this?
What is it that afflicts you?

BERTHA.

Nay, forgive me!
Speak gently to me, Leonhard: I am not
In sorrow, but I felt somewhat less cheerful
Than I am wont to be,—perchance the music
Of yesternight: that ballad was most plaintive;
It made me weep then, and its haunting tones

Came o'er my heart this morning, and the tears
Sprang forth against my will.

LEONHARD.

A weak excuse.
You've lost your cheerfulness for some time past.
You scarce repay me, Bertha, for the care
I give to you unceasingly,—as though
You had become my child as well as wife.
Beware, lest this weak fancy grow upon you.

BERTHA.

Nay, I am not unthankful for your love,
And that I call my daily life to witness.
Forgive me, Leonhard! I am to blame.
You are all care for one who is unworthy
To have a guardian gifted like yourself:
But I am not so highly wrought as those
Who have a fuller measure dealt to them.
'Twas never mine to gaze on earth or heaven,
Nor know I how a lofty soul like yours

Can brook the bondage you have taken on you.
And yet, sometimes, I think you minister
With eyes that patience brightens more than love.
Oh, Leonhard! do you love me as you did
When first you talked to me of love, and sealed
Those vows, which I drank in so eagerly,
With that sweet kiss? Oh, Leonhard! let your heart
Answer for me; and if your love is less,
It must be for some grievous fault of mine.
Oh, tell me what it is? and I will strive
To mend the imperfection. I have eased
My heart, and breathe again. Oh, speak, dear love!
Your silence is more terrible to me,
Than e'en your sternest chiding.

LEONHARD.

I am not
Displeased with you, my Bertha; but much grieved
To think your idle fancies wrong me thus.
Ah, how unlike the hours we used to spend
Together! and the contrast strikes my heart

With more of anguish than I can express.
It is no fault of mine; my conscience gives
No harsh reproach, for I have felt the care
I took upon me cheerfully, no less
A sacred trust; and when at times, perchance
Suffering from ills which come upon us all,
I've felt unlike myself, the sense of duty
Has nerved my heart, and given me strength again.

BERTHA.

I knew it, Leonhard—knew it must be so;
You've felt it as a task—an irksome one!
Yes, now I know it all; your love is bent
Beneath the load, and duty has been forced
To spur the jaded spirit to its task!
Oh, Leonhard! I feel I've lived too long.

LEONHARD.

Bertha, why vex me thus? I feel a sense
Of anger in my heart ne'er felt before,
And know, moreover, that my anger's just.

I never said you were a weary task.
'Tis clear you love me not, and your changed heart
Reflects on mine ; but you may live to know
You've wronged me, Bertha : think upon this more,
And you will feel you have been much to blame.
I leave you till you've dried your foolish tears.

BERTHA.

Oh ! do not leave me : wait a little while.
I hear fair Julia's voice : be kind to me,—
Forgive me, dearest Leonhard ! Do not say
Aught that can lead her to suspect this scene :
I will be gay again.

LEONHARD.

So Julia leaves
The castle in a few short days. Have you
Pressed her to stay, as courtesy demands ?

BERTHA.

I did so press her ; but she has received

Letters from Heidelberg, which move her much.
Her brother, whom she has not seen for years,
Is there, and writes to her most earnestly
To make a swift return. Perhaps your voice
May have more weight.

LEONHARD.

Nay, let her go. I named
The matter merely that she might not leave
Without receiving all due courtesy.

BERTHA.

I grieve she's going. I shall miss her much;
But having you, dear Leonhard, I feel
I have the world! The day is fine and dry;
You promised you would take me to the steep,
And read to me this afternoon. Dear Leonhard,
May I remind you of the promised joy?

LEONHARD.

I shall be ready to attend you then.

Meanwhile, dear Bertha, let no foolish whims
Disturb the surface of your happiness.

[*Exeunt.*

SCENE III.—*Another Room in the Castle.*

JULIA *and* EMMELINE.

JULIA.

Remember, Emmeline, you're pledged to write
At least once every week.

EMMELINE.

I will not fail.
I would the claims were not so very urgent
That call you from us, as the Spring approaches.
The Lady Bertha and the Count will feel
Your absence, for you made us gay again.

JULIA.

I made you gay?

EMMELINE.

Ah ! certainly you did.
When first the Count was married to my lady,
He seemed to live alone when she was near him,
And he was ministering to her smallest wants.
I lost my occupation on a sudden ;
The Count wrote all her letters—read all to her—
Led her from room to room ; his arm became
What mine had been ; and when the sky was fair,
And the birds warbled like a world of lovers,
He led her to the terrace, where she sat,
And he beside her. Sometimes they would go
To the green slope that looks upon the glen,
Just where the trees stretch out a canopy
Of rustling boughs, which ever and anon
Waving, let fall a flickering gleam of light :
There he would read to her, and while away
The morning hours in sweet love-talk. Sometimes,
When I have come upon them unawares,
Her half-flushed cheek has been prest close to his ;
While his fond arm has held in willing thraldom

Her slender waist: doubtless he felt her heart
Beat quickly on it. Well, after a time
He gave me somewhat of my duties back;
Which made me feel glad as a worshipper,
Whose saint returns to an old shrine again.
Then by degrees the Count walked by himself,
Rode out, and read in silence: he complained
That reading out aloud fatigued him much,
And made him sore at throat.

JULIA.

Indeed! But how
Bore this the Lady Bertha?

EMMELINE.

As a saint
Who lives in love and patience, caring for
Another's comfort only, not her own,
Until you came, my lady's earliest friend,
And the Count's love, or rather, I should say,
His anxious care to please his wife returned

Most suddenly. He read again, and—but you know
Full well the tenour of their daily life.

JULIA.

I think you must have fancied the Count grew
Remiss in his attention to your lady;
For I have watched him narrowly, and gazed
With admiration on his tenderness.
Nor can I see how my arrival here
Could have brought back these daily walks: you wrong
Count Leonhard by the thought.

EMMELINE.

You give a wrong
Meaning to my words: of all men I know,
Count Leonhard is the noblest and the gentlest,
And I shall love him for my lady's sake.
I do not blame him for his growing tired
Of love-walks. Honeymoons can't last for ever:
They seldom last a month. An aunt once told me
They come and perish sometimes in a day,—
Nay, often in an hour! So said my aunt;

But she is an old maid : those envious creatures
Hate weddings as they do a handsome face.
I wonder what can make old maids so spiteful !

JULIA.

Resolve yourself the doubt : what makes you so ?
You are unmarried, therefore an old maid.

EMMELINE.

No, not an old one yet. Surely there's time
For me to marry, for I am not thirty.

JULIA.

Good Emmeline, before you rail again
At all old maids, we'll wait to see how far
We are upon the sunny side of youth ;
Remember, too, they live apart from joy,
Nor taste the sweet calamity of love.

EMMELINE.

But I must leave you now, my Lady Julia :

I have to send young Wilfred to the village,
On some kind errand from the Count.

[*Exit* Emmeline.

JULIA.

That girl is truly worth her weight in gold.
She is the sweetest tempered soul alive,
And shrewd withal. I am more loath to leave
Than I should wish her to suspect: my heart
Clings to this spot, as though it were my home.
How chafed the Count was, when I went to him:
What could have roused him thus? 'Tis not his wont
To speak of Bertha so: no man alive
Loves his wife more. At times, deep study seems
To weave a glittering fancy in his brain,
Which turns him from his nature; yet his heart
Is noble and humane. Perchance 't may be
The consciousness that all his wealth and state
Came to him by his wife. He's somewhat proud,
And over sensitive.

[*Exit.*

SCENE IV.—*A retired Part of the Domains, near the Brow of the Precipice.*

Enter BERTHA *and* LEONHARD.

BERTHA.

Dear Leonhard, will you never speak to me?
Why are you silent? Hear you not the birds
Sing in the branches their sweet melodies?
Surely you love me. Has this favourite spot
No pleasant charm? Do you remember, love,
That here we first exchanged those happy vows
Which made me yours for ever? Here your lips
First sealed them with a kiss. I often dream
I'm sitting near the precipice, where once
You told me the sad tale of Rosamond,
And how she perished for her love. 'Twere sweet
To die for one we loved,—oh, very sweet!
Come, take me to that seat upon the steep,
Where we will sit, and you shall tell again
Some legend of the past. —

LEONHARD, *about to speak, stops, then remains lost in thought: after a pause,*

What was it that you said, my dearest Bertha?
Oh! that you wished to sit where once I told you
The history of Fair Rosamond! We'll go.
We are not near the spot; so you can walk
Forward in safety. On, I'll follow you.

BERTHA.

Follow close to me, dearest Leonhard.
Come, sweetest, follow me!

[Bertha *walks slowly on, and exit.*

LEONHARD, *regarding her with agitation, approaches the side of the scene where she left,*

Oh, God! she's fallen o'er the precipice!

[*Looks hurriedly round, and rushes out in the opposite direction.*

NOTE.

A period of five years is supposed to elapse between the fourth and fifth Acts.

ACT V.

SCENE I.—*Part of the Grounds on the Count's Estate.*

Enter KARL, ANSELM, CONRAD, &c.

CONRAD.

WELL, Anselm! it will be a glorious day:
'Tis many a year since we have had such doings.
Why, let me see,—not since our lady died,
And that's five years to-morrow.

ANSELM.

Five years to-day, you mean.

CONRAD.

Nay, *to-morrow*, I say.

ANSELM.

I tell you *'tis* to-day! You're thinking on

The morn we found her lying in the dell :
She met her fate the day before. Remember,
We searched all night for her !

CONRAD.

Ay, you are right.
I meant 'tis five years since the day we found her :
I date from that. I never shall forget
How my lord looked, when first he heard the news :
He never has recovered that rude shock.
Time, that wears down the grief of other men
And plants the smiles again, with him has set
The seal of sadness deeper on his brow.
We never see him smile now ; Lady Julia
Has caught his sorrow. Why, she's gloomy too !

ANSELM.

And yet, if ever man deserved a life
Brimful of happiness, it is the Count.
He is the best and noblest man alive.
It makes me sad to think how sad he is :

He has no pleasure in his former sports;
No hunting now, no archery, no games,
No dances with soft music of the night!
Well, but we are to have a festival,
And so I hope a joyful change 's at hand.

CONRAD.

No doubt of it: perchance he meant to mourn
Five years, and then throw off his sorrowings.
Some men have foolish fancies; yet I hold
That mourning for a wife is virtuous,—
Yea, very proper, and almost religious.
The man's a knave else. When my first wife died,
I thought that I should never laugh again,
And meant to die as quickly as I could.
I don't know how it was, but every day
Made the grief less; and then my little girl,
Jacyntha, prattled of her mother, which
Made me weep often and relieved my heart.
Time's a great wearer down of grief. Then I had to work
For every bit of bread we ate. I bless
My God, who has dispensed my portion thus;

For had I been as wealthy as my lord,
I might have mourned like him, and been as wretched.
Yet it was long ere I could go to work
Upon my garden, after my day's toil,
Till one eve, looking for a favourite rose-tree
Of my poor wife's, I found it choked with weeds;
And so I went to work, and half reproached
Myself I'd left her flowers so long neglected;
Ah, occupation is the cure for grief!

ANSELM.

Ah! ah! we know the rest. You fell in love
Again, and married the old butler's daughter;
And now you are as gay as ever.

CONRAD.

True:
And yet I love not my first wife the less,—
Nay, love her more, e'en as a saint in heaven!
I often pray to her, and never see
Aught that reminds me of her, but I bless
Her name and memory from my very heart!

ANSELM.

Why, man, you're crying now: there's gladness for you!
You are as foolish as my lord.

CONRAD.

Nay, mine are tears of love. God bless her heart!
And I must tell my little wife of this,
For she loves Gertrude too.

ANSELM.

No more of this. Let us away and make
The myrtle arch, 'neath which our lady sits
To give the prizes to the men to-morrow.
But never, while you live, reproach the Count
Because he mourns the Lady Bertha, since
Your eyes are red with weeping for your wife,
Who has been dead much longer than your lord's.
You are a pretty man to lecture him!

CONRAD.

All is over now; but if you speak of her

Five years to come, I shall then weep again.
I feel as though the tears, in spite of me,
Would flow for her, who's now a saint in heaven.

ANSELM.

Well, I may marry if I grow a fool,
And so I won't laugh any more at you.
Come, let's away; we have no little work
Before the sun goes down behind the hills.

[*Exeunt.*

SCENE II.—*The Count's Study.—Night.*

The Room hung round with the Pictures of old German Warriors, the Ancestors of the Lady Bertha.

LEONHARD.

Five years? Great God! it must be centuries.
Oh, what a weary length is life! Yet I
Have seen but half the years doled out to man.

All nature seems to crawl along in pain.
I have infected it, and hung a shroud
Upon the visible glory of the world,
Changing the stars to ashes. How the wind,
That moaning voice of night, howls round the turrets,
As though it bore a death-shriek stifled in
The depths of its unfathomable tongue!
Not an hour creeps but I do register it
With some fierce pang, that brands its memory
In fire upon the tablet of my brain.
Why one would deem the human heart must stop
Beneath the weight which hangs on every pulse,
And that the mind would grow confused and dull
With this unsleeping vigil of my thought,
Brooding like Satan on the throne of hell!
How long is't since I've had a moment's peace?
And what is peace? Ah! that I only know
But that I have it not.
I have had feverish moments of delight,
And lost for some short time the sense of woe
By rushing into pleasure; but oh, peace!

Calm, sweet-souled peace! that left me with a sigh
Which seemed like parting from a heavenly guest,
When first I trod the burning path of passion.
Passion is brief, and dies; but from its grave
Rises a mighty demon, strong to curse,
The vampire fiend—Remorse, which lives on crime,
Till by degrees the struggling spirit writhes
Beneath the clinging of its twining flames
Like Laocoon, in serpent folds fast wreathed.
Guilt is a leprosy to every thought,—
Makes memory a hell, and hope a fear;
Turns daylight into torture, gives to night
A silence far more terrible than day,
With her accusing voices.

My own voice sounds
Like to a judge who, on a seat which groans
Beneath the weight of his own conscious crimes,
Dooms some poor maddened homicide to die
For blind revenge, while he feels every word
Strike on his heart self-condemnation!
Not midnight yet? Is there no day to come?

Will an eternal darkness rest on time,
With intermittent flashes of a storm
Alone to show us what we hate to see?
Faith is a fearless thing. Once in the night
When, like a serpent by an angel's side,
I lay by Bertha, suddenly there came
A tempest roaring through the waste of heaven;
The crash of thunders bursting o'er my head
Scared sleep away. I started up; a flood
Of fiery lightning rushed across my sight.
I closed my eyes in horrible dismay!
Again the thunders revelled in a roar
Which shook the murky vault. Aghast I fell
Back on my pillow, like a trembling wretch
Who begs for mercy crouching to a fiend;
While that sweet soul, calm in her innocence
And strong in faith, said, in her starry voice,
"I trust no peasant is abroad to-night."

[*The turret clock strikes.*

'Tis midnight now:
Each clangy stroke a separate death-knell sounds,

And has a meaning for mine ear which those
Who count the chimings at a gallant masque
Would shudder but to dream of; and I go
From day to day beneath this dreary load,
Till it a natural burthen seems.

Oh! for some spot
Where I could lie and gasp my life away
Beneath the stupifying drowse of death!
And as my spirit fell into the dark,
Some gleaming god would say, with soothing voice,
The past's a dream, the future is a sleep
Without a dream, and thou, dead thought, art nothing.
Oh, joyful thought! Its passage through my brain,
So populous with agonies, has lulled
The household pangs that dwell and reign therein.

[*after a pause.*

Sleep has no love for me, nor I for it.
Remorse then revels, holds a ghastly court,
Is a gaunt monarch crowned with a death's head
Throned on a ruined heart; while I, spell-bound,
Inhale with greedy mouth a burning feast.

[*Takes up a book, turns over the leaves listlessly, and then throws it down in disgust.*

This page I've read to her a thousand times,
And now it open sprang as though alive,
To curse me with its presence! Sorrowful
And vain the labour spent in old pursuits,
However once enjoyed, once prized, once loved,
When a guilt-stricken spirit turns the leaves.
Oh! what a contrast to the joys that were,
But are not now. The glow of Poesie
Has died away: Apollo's laurels hang
All withered, down a sad and tear-worn face;
His kindling glance has gone, his harp is broken;
The music has departed, and the voice
Comes like the haunting memories of a ghost,
Which has no rest in an unquiet grave.
Thought rolls on thought, as black and sluggish throes
Which have no shore to rest their toiling on,
No sand to die on, like a weary wave
That ever labouring, moaning, heaving on,
Is part of the eternal, restless sea.

What a glad thing a ragged beggar is !
The man who yesterday asked alms of me,
As I was loitering near the Rolandspeck,
Lost in a vision of my earlier days,
Seemed like a *man:* his look was bold and free;
Joy was a plant firm-rooted in his heart,
Putting its leaves and flowers forth to the sky
And sunbright air. I saw it,—marked it well,
By the strong quiet of his steadfast eye;
And as I flung a golden coin, it seemed
A world to him. Alas! how little he
Supposed the wealthy donor groaned within
That he was not *the beggar!* Rank, power, wealth,
Are but accumulations of despair
And active miseries to guilty souls!
Beggars alone are happy. Night has stars,
And day has sunshine for them,—all is good.

[*Looks up, and fixes his eye on a picture of a German warrior, ancestor of* Bertha.

How horribly that warrior scowls on me
The torture of that dull and fixed dead-stare,

Searching with shrouded gaze into my heart,
Like to a fiend who has the hate of hell,—
The justice of a god! A painter there
Stood for a few short hours, and plied his hands,
Active with malice, and upon the wall
Left that dead face to blast me! But I could
Rip it to shreds, and in a moment's time,
With this sharp steel of mine, now bared before me.
And yet I pause: I dare not strike a picture,
For fear of something standing armed behind
That fragile canvas. Hah! the picture moves!
No; it was but my fancy: yet the eyes
Have all the venom of a human look.

Enter JULIA, *in her night-dress.*

What noise is that? [*sees* Julia.
Bertha! and from her grave! Alive in death!
Avaunt, and spare me! spare your——

[*He rises from his seat, totters towards her, sinks down apparently dead, striking his head against an oak carved cherub.*

JULIA.

Oh, heaven ! My dearest Leonhard !
Leonhard ! Leonhard !
[*stooping down and taking his hand.*

LEONHARD, *recovering himself.*

Oh, Julia, such a dream ! How came I here ?
How came *you* here ?

JULIA.

How pale you look : there's blood upon your face.

LEONHARD, *frantickly.*

Blood ! Whose blood ? Bertha's blood ?
I have betrayed myself. *(aside.)*
(aloud.) What have I said ?
What have I said ? Julia, repeat to me [*to* Julia.
Each word I uttered now,—quick, every word !

JULIA.

Look not so wild, dear Leonhard. What frenzy

Has come upon the quiet of your brain,
And turned your thought to violence?
Not an hour since I left you reading here,
And then you said you soon would come to rest.

LEONHARD, *faintly.*

What have I said? Tell me what I have said.
You found me dreaming, did you not?
What said I in my dream?

JULIA.

I know not what you said. A confused sound
Such as the sleeping utter; nothing more.
But what makes you so curious to know
The rambling speeches of an idle dream?
Dearest, you're ill. Let us retire, my love;
Sleep will soon bring you to your calm again.

[Leonhard, *who seems paralysed, takes* Julia's *hand, and slowly exeunt.*

SCENE III.—*A Hall in the Castle.—Morning.*

Enter LEONHARD *and his* STEWARD, *talking.*

LEONHARD.

I tell thee, sirrah, that the lazy knaves
Eye me as though they longed to wag their tongues
In saucy parle: the rogues have nought to do,
And so they run to ruin. Let me have
The castle clear of them before I sleep.
Send them away, for I will cleanse my house
Of these most pestilent rascals. Why, you stare
As though you were a fool! D'ye hear me, dolt?

STEWARD.

My good lord, but consider——

LEONHARD.

Did you not hear me speak?
Go, and perform my bidding.

STEWARD.

My good lord,
Dismiss your servants ! What am I to do ?
Who will attend upon your lordship then ?
Which of them shall I send away ?

LEONHARD.

All, fellow, all !

STEWARD.

What reason shall I give them for the step ?
So sudden, too. My noble master, pause
One minute.

LEONHARD.

Not for an instant. Reason ?
Give them my reasons ? Why, it is my will,
And that is cause sufficient. Idle knaves,
They want to know my reasons ! They have incurred
Your lady's censure ; that is cause enough.

And when has Power ever deigned to give
A reason for its dealings! Might is right:
I know I have found it so. *(aside.)* Sirrah, away.!
Linger not here, but clear my house of them.

STEWARD.

Had you not better wait, my lord, till I
Have hired fresh servants in their stead?

LEONHARD.

Begone! thou obstinate fellow, or I'll send
Thee packing with them.
[*Exit* Steward.
Now is one dark weight lifted from my heart,
And I shall breathe more freely after this:
Their busy prying eyes are now removed.
With what a weary crawling o'er the ground
Guilt, in its very highest pleasure, walks!
Where will these varlets go? That had escaped
The blindness of my rage. If scarcely here,
Beneath the very battery of my frown,

I fancy they suspect me, and discourse
Of that unhappy deed, what will they not
Dare to affirm—and swear, when they are sent
Thus hastily away, enraged by this
Sudden dismissal? Shall I cast them forth
To sow all Germany with suspicious doubts,
For me to reap the harvest of their venom?
Oh, no; that must not be! They'd better stay,
Caged in this hell of mine, for me to bear
The sharpest pangs of their accusing eyes,
Than let them roam to preach it all abroad.
I must prevent this,—yea, and stop the tongue
Of Caspar, so that these shrewd knaves may not
Know what has passed. Oh, what a curse is guilt!
That it should drag an immortal spirit down
From the high pinnacle of its loftiest will,
To crouch and tremble like a beaten hound,
And lick the dust before its menials' feet!

Re-enter STEWARD.

What now?

STEWARD.

Your reverend kinsman, the Bishop of Cologne,
Desires a conference with you.

LEONHARD.

Admit him straight to me. Touching the matter
I named to you just now, do not proceed
Further in it; and mark me, not a word
Of my displeasure to your fellow-servants.
Go, find them work to do. Ask the Bishop in.
[*Exit* Steward.
What can he want with me? 'Tis many a day
Since I have seen him. Doubtless he comes
To ask for offerings to the church.

Enter Bishop.

Most welcome, reverend kinsman. I am much
Indebted to the occasion of your visit.

BISHOP.

My son, I come to spare you trouble,
And save you from collision with the State.

LEONHARD.

Collision with the State! What mean you, Father?

BISHOP.

There is a murderer harboured on your lands,
Whom the State now demands of you through me;
For in consideration of your rank,
And the good service you have done the Duke,
I come now to expostulate with you.

LEONHARD, *agitated.*

A murderer, say you? Who is the murderer?
Where is the witness? Who accuses me?

BISHOP.

I marvel much, and grieve that you, my son,
Who stand so highly in the world's esteem,
So famed for gentleness and virtuous deeds,
Should screen a murderer from the hands of justice.
Twice has the State demanded this vile man,

This monster stained with his wife's innocent blood,
This Ernst, who basks in your protection here.

LEONHARD.

Great God, how blind is guilt! I'd nearly let
My guilty secret out, fool that I was! *(aside.)*
Most dear and reverend kinsman, it is true
The State has twice demanded this poor wretch,
This Ernst, who is, they say, bestained with blood;
But I was pledged, before I knew his crime,
To shelter him, by a true German's oath,
And he is penitent—nay, let him live
To expiate his crime. Be sure of this,
He suffers more than vengeance can inflict.

BISHOP.

The law must judge of that. As for your oath,
It is unlawful; and you are not bound
To stand by vows, when thus by fraud extorted.

LEONHARD.

Father, I hoped to find you on the side

Of mercy. Can you bring the dead to life
By this man's slaughter? Rather, do you not
Follow his fearful step, most foul example,
And seek to cure one murder by another,—
And without provocation? He in rage,
Blinded by passion, takes no heed of life:
The law in calm cold malice slakes its thirst
Of blood, by showing that it also has
No reverence for life.

BISHOP.

That sounds more like
The special pleading of a man, who is
Himself a murderer, than the calm dictate
Of your own judgment.

LEONHARD.

What mean you, reverend Father?
I do not set so lightly by an oath,
As you would seem to do.

BISHOP.

My noble kinsman,
I make one more appeal to you. You may
Reflect discredit, compromise your honour,
By interposing your unsullied fame
Between the law and a foul criminal.

LEONHARD.

We are all criminals in the sight of God.
But since you think, good Father, I am bound
To put aside my oath, the sin is yours.
He shall be given up unto the State:
Will this content you?

BISHOP.

I had hoped no less
From one of your severe morality.
Farewell! my son.

LEONHARD.

Good Father, fare you well!
[*Exit* Bishop.

It must be so; for had I longer stood
In opposition to the State, it might
Have drawn suspicion on myself, and not
Saved him,—my brother murderer. I will straight
Go to him, bid him quickly fly, and give
Some gold to the poor wretch. Perchance
He may repent; though if he feel what I
Incessantly endure, he'd better plunge
A dagger in his heart, and fly to God
At once for His decision: heaven, or hell!

[*Exit, hastily.*

SCENE IV.—*An Apartment in the Castle.*

JULIA *and* EMMELINE.

JULIA.

I will put faith in your presentiment,
And hope that henceforth we shall be more cheerful:
But sorrows that have been with us so long
Must slowly die away, not all at once
Fly like a startled swallow from its nest.

EMMELINE.

Dear lady, grief may be a household guest
For many years, yet on a sudden die.
Think you a wife, whose husband has been held
In drear captivity, while she bewailed
Her desolation, takes an age to grow
Glad at his coming, when some Autumn eve
His voice, like long-lost music, meets her ear,
And ere her eye can reassure her reason,
Their hearts beat quick and loudly 'gainst each other ?
Or when a mother, who for months has hung
Over an infant's couch, while fever drained
Her dear child's life away; think you, when health
Like a returning tide flows back, there needs
Deep thought to teach her heart to feel its joy ?
Believe me, lady, in the glad sunshine,
Night-fears with darkness die.

JULIA.

Well, I will try
To tutor my sad face to wear a smile,
And, if I can, my heart.

EMMELINE.

Nay, if you fight against a coming joy,
It e'en may turn away: no golden moth
Bears handling less than pleasure. Remember this,
The Grand Duke comes to-morrow: we shall have
A happy day at least,—a good beginning
For the Count's restoration to his wits.

JULIA, *angrily.*

Emmeline, you forget yourself.

EMMELINE.

Your pardon!
I should say to his mirth. But is it not
A marvel, passing my poor wit to clear,
That one so full of noble gifts should let
A constant sadness wear his heart away?
How strangely, too, does it infect us all!
I sometimes catch myself in tears; but now
I know as surely all will soon be changed,
As though we had a festival each day,
With rustic dances to fill up the night.

Let me propose to you, dear lady, while
The project 's in my brain, to urge my lord
To spend a day in that sweet little isle
That stands midway in the Rhine's noble stream;
I mean that with the chapel.

JULIA.

We will talk
Of your proposal when this fête is o'er;
Surely, good Emmeline, one fête 's enough
To please you at a time: you would be gay indeed.

EMMELINE.

Day closes with bright promise for the morrow.
What dress mean you to wear?

JULIA.

I care not: e'en the first that comes to hand.

EMMELINE.

Then let me choose.

JULIA.

I cannot have a better taste than yours.
But, surely, these are things scarce worth a thought.

EMMELINE.

Indeed they are. Old Bridget told Wilhelmine
She would bestow a marriage-gift worth gold.
The gift was this,—a piece of good advice:
"When you are married, pretty Wilhelmine,
Dress with as much solicitude as though
You had to charm a lover's eye: most girls
Can gain the lover, few can please the husband."
Therefore I will search out your wedding-dress.

JULIA.

It has been seldom worn,—I scarce know when.

EMMELINE.

Were I a wife, I'd wear it every day.
When 'twas worn out, I'd have another made
So like it, that I'd cheat my husband's eyes.

JULIA.

A faithful wife indeed, to cheat your husband.
You are a worthy monitor, forsooth!

EMMELINE.

Nay, only cheat him to his own delight.

JULIA.

'Tis growing late. I wonder much the Count
Has not returned: it must be far beyond
The accustomed time.

EMMELINE.

He's busy, doubtless, with
The workmen in the grounds.

JULIA.

Nay, that can't be.
He told me the arrangements were complete.
Go, Emmeline, seek Caspar, and ask him
If he has seen the Count.

[*Exit* Emmeline.

JULIA, *throwing open the casement.*

A lovely night indeed: the happy stars
Shine out, as though they were angelic eyes
Looking on earth with more than human love.
And yet they tell us earth's a glorious star!
Still, who can think those globes of throbbing light
To which our eyes turn up so longingly,
Gilding our saddest tears, and raising thought
Midway to the blue heavens, are, in truth,
Worlds like our own, and full of wretchedness,—
The dark abodes of sin? If they are worlds,
They must be worlds of joy, perchance the homes
Of angels, or of beings who have passed
Through human trial here, and who at last
Rest there secure from weariness or change.

[*The sound of music is heard.*

That music must be from the Jager band
Which is to play before the Duke to-morrow.
Night is the time for music, for 'tis then
The past and future meet the present hour
Beneath the spell of song, which brings a dream

Like to a golden cloud around the heart,
So full of fond regret and tearful hope,
That e'en the desolate feel a touch of joy
Which seems a memory of paradise,
Or else a hope of heaven.

[*Scene closes.*]

SCENE V.—*Near the Precipice. Time, Evening.*

LEONHARD *enters slowly.*

The night is drawing on. I know not why
I linger in the grounds, for it is chill,
And the dews fall like to the damps of death ;
The winds hang funeral dirges on the trees,
And the mists rise from earth, or fall from heaven.
At this still hour,—how many gasp their last
Of life away, unconscious of the ebb
Of that great tide, which leaves them fixed for ever
On that dark shore, the peopled realm of death !

To-morrow's sun will rise on many a frame
That's warm to-night, but will be cold to-morrow,
Serene and marble-like, with fallen lips
And the blank eye fixed in death's cold-blind stare.
I seem to-night to gloat upon the thought
Of death. Oh, God! I would this night had passed,
But above all, the morrow! I rejoice
Over the flight of every passing day,
As though I were a steed who had to run
On fire until he reached the far-off goal.
How can I bear the mockery of the fête?
How welcome with a gay and smiling face
Our Duke, who honours with his princely train
My castle? Mine?—Bertha's it was, and is,—
Not mine. Five years to-morrow—nay, to-day,
Upon this very spot she left my arm
At my accursed bidding, "Go, I'll follow you!"
Cowardly liar! brutal, offal slave!
Oh, guileless suicide, what a shock was that!
Walking in calm reliance on my word
And full of faith, she fell from earth to heaven.

Her voice and form have haunted me all day;
She has been walking by my side; I've turned
My head around to look at her. Oh, that I
Could blot that fatal hour from memory, when
Remorse, a poisoned arrow, struck my heart!
One crime, and all my life is dark! I am a weed!
God! Thou hast dealt *justly,* not gently with me.
Gently with *me?* How did I deal with her?
Oh, *'tis* just! for as a shadow dogs a shape
With the full sun before it, so does suffering
Follow the steps of guilt. Yet, surely, I
Have claims on heavenly mercy. I have sought
The wretched out, and made them glad again.
The widow and the orphan bless me; and the crowd
Say, as I pass, "There goes the good Count Leonhard,
The kind and generous!" Oh, could they see
The workings of my heart, they would recoil
Back with affright, and shuddering say, "There goes
A blood-stained murderer!"

I cannot nerve
Myself for all to-morrow's mockery

Of gladness, while a dark heart groans within;
Nor will I. I must end this curse to-night,—
And *here!* What voice was that? The rocks
Hold in their black and stony ears the words
Which take possession of my soul and brain,—
"Go on, I'll follow!" See! they gaze at me,
And fancy puts a Gorgon look on each.
And I will follow thee, thou murdered saint!
This deed shall wipe that wretched murder out.
I will devote myself, like them of old,
To the infernal gods, and from the steep
Plunge into blank oblivion: that will end
The dread ordeal! Nay, but it might tell
The guilty secret. What of that? I shall
Be far beyond the reach of friend or foe,
Beyond the hiss of scorn, the scowl of hate.
Let them pile contumely on my corpse,
And mock the calm of death,—deny me burial;
What's that to me? Oh, that the mountain kites
Would tear me limb from limb, and feed their brood
With my detested flesh, so that no trace

Of this most wretched being might remain !
Perchance there might from this spring forth a tale
Like that which gilds the fratricidal name
Of Rome's great tyrant founder, who, when slain
By his rude senators, was taken out
Piecemeal, concealed within their flowing robes,
For secret burial : yet the mob believed
He had been snatched to heaven as a god !
I pause, and have not heart enough to throw
These atoms to oblivion. Am I grown
Coward, as well as murderer ? Am I sunk
So low in degradation ? Leonhard
Arise, and be a man ! I call you from
The pit of your abasement. Had you heart
To lay a snare, by which a guileless soul,
Who would have walked on ocean at your word,
Fell in without a struggle, and you draw
Back with affright ? I, who have ate her bread ?
Made affluent by her murder ? Merciless deed,
To slay a benefactor ! I am grown
A paltry craven ; even now my knees

Shake like the aspen, and my curdling flesh
Has a cold dew upon it. No way left
But this appalling leap? Down, Leonhard, down
On penitential knees! Confess your sins;
Howl to your God for mercy; kneel at once,—
Christ's blood will wash that guilty stain away.
He died for you; renounce your hardened state,
Throw off the haughty man, and be a child!
Surely some angel whispers to my soul;
But roaring Hell with all his voices drowns
The blessèd monitor. The air seems thronged
With staring fiends dipped in a sea of blood;
I gasp for breath, and fire roars down my throat!
A madness bursts upon my brain, which reels
A blazing ruin; the ruddy stars
Curse me with blinking eyes! The rocks cry out—
"Go on, I'll follow thee!" One prayer to God!
Oh, Christ! the demons choke me with their shrieks.
I cannot pray:—the world seems red with blood!
She had no time for prayer,—she needed none;
But I——back, fiends of hell! press not on me!
They hem me in—and try to strangle me.

Avaunt, ye hell-hounds! give me room to breathe.
Pursue me if you will. My brain's on fire!
"Bertha, I follow thee!" [*rushes out.*

SCENE VI.—*An Apartment in the Castle. Time, the early Dawn.*

JULIA, *alone; watching anxiously, and pacing her Chamber.*

'Tis long past midnight; and no tidings yet
Of Leonhard. My heart grows like a weight
Of lead: some evil has befallen him,—
Perchance a sudden fit. Now I remember,
He has of late oft prest his hand to his head
And closed his eyes, as though the blood were mounting
Quick to his brain. Will day-light never spring
From out the east? That tardy star has hung
Above the starting-place of day, till I
Ache at its beauty, and abhor its brightness.
Ah! it grows paler, and a purple flush
Came out, as from a furnace opened wide!

Another golden flood; the star is drowned
In the wide-spreading sea of light. 'Tis morn;
The birds are singing, and the sluggish mists
Roll churlishly away.

I will go now
Upon the terrace, and await the coming
Of the domestics,—dare I hope the Count?
He may have lost his way. The darkness fell
Like a black mantle upon earth last night;
Pray Heaven he may have missed his path, and found
A shelter in some peasant's home.

Enter EMMELINE.

EMMELINE.

Dear lady,
From the old turret I espy them coming.
Oh! they have found the Count; they'd never else
So soon return.

JULIA.

Thank Heaven! Let us at once
Go on the terrace. [*Exeunt.*

SCENE VII.—*A Dell, the Precipice rising above it. Time, the early Morning.*

COUNT LEONHARD *discovered lying at the bottom of the steep.*

Enter CASPAR, CONRAD, ANSELM, RUDOLPH, *and other Domestics.*

RUDOLPH.

'Twere better we returned. We've searched the village,
The woods and fields, yet cannot find the Count.

ANSELM.

A sorry tale to tell the Lady Julia.

CONRAD.

I'm weary unto death: but still I'd roam
The whole world through to find our noble Count.

ANSELM.

Ah, me! I cannot counsel what to do:
We have not left a single nook unsearched.

RUDOLPH.

We now must hasten to the castle home;
We may chance find him there.

MICHAEL.

Pray Heaven it be so! But let's return.

[*As he is turning back to pass the end of the dell, he sees the body of the Count.*

Look, Rudolph, look! Here is the Count at last,
And lying fast asleep.

RUDOLPH.

Hush! Anselm, look!
He is fast locked in sleep.

ANSELM, *after a pause.*

Too still for sleep!

RUDOLPH, *approaching close to the Count.*

Great God! there's blood upon his head. My lord!
He moves not. He has sure been murdered here.

See! what a gash is on his forehead. Help!
[*They all draw round the body, and raise it.*

ANSELM, *touching the face.*

Alas! he's dead: his face is clammy cold.
He must have fallen o'er the precipice.
Oh, our poor lady! What a dreadful tale!

RUDOLPH.

I always thought he would repent, some day,
Walking so often near that giddy height!

CASPAR.

The very spot on which our lady fell,—
I mean the Lady Bertha. The poor Count
Has never been the man he was since she,
Sweet lady, met with her untimely end.
We've never seen him smile since that sad day.
Dear Heaven! he has been thinking of her fate,
And, blind with tears, unconscious of the brink,
Fallen o'er, and shared her frightful death too well.

A sorry sight! a woful day! Alas,
We never shall behold so good a man!
You well may weep: we've lost our kindest friend.
There will not be one tearless eye in Bonn,
When this is noised abroad. A woful day!

MICHAEL.

Well, let us bear his body to the castle,
Poor Lady Julia! Our kind, good master!
Rudolph must tell the melancholy tale,
For I am sure I could not for my tears.

[*Exeunt, bearing off the body.*

THE END.

LONDON:
Printed by Maurice & Co., Howford-buildings,
Fenchurch-street.

118

book should be returned to the
n or before the last date stamped

ne of five cents a day is incurred by
beyond the specified time.

Check Out More Titles From HardPress Classics Series In this collection we are offering thousands of classic and hard to find books. This series spans a vast array of subjects – so you are bound to find something of interest to enjoy reading and learning about.

Subjects:
Architecture
Art
Biography & Autobiography
Body, Mind &Spirit
Children & Young Adult
Dramas
Education
Fiction
History
Language Arts & Disciplines
Law
Literary Collections
Music
Poetry
Psychology
Science
…and many more.

Visit us at www.hardpress.net

Im The Story
personalised classic books

"Beautiful gift.. lovely finish.
My Niece loves it, so precious!"
Helen R Brumfieldon

UNIQUE GIFT
FOR KIDS, PARTNERS AND FRIENDS

Timeless books such as:

Kids

Alice in Wonderland • The Jungle Book • The Wonderful Wizard of Oz
Peter and Wendy • Robin Hood • The Prince and The Pauper
The Railway Children • Treasure Island • A Christmas Carol

Adults

Romeo and Juliet • Dracula

Highly Customizable
Change Books Title
Replace Characters Names with yours
Upload Photo (for inside page)
Add Inscriptions

Visit
Im The Story.com
and order yours today!

* 9 7 8 0 4 6 1 4 1 4 9 1 2 *

SD - #0018 - 290622 - C0 - 229/152/10 - PB - 9780461414912 - Gloss Lamination